I AM AUTISTIC
A WORKBOOK

Sensory Tools, Practical Advice, and Interactive Journaling for Understanding Life with Autism (by Someone Diagnosed with It)

Written and illustrated
by Chanelle Moriah

ULYSSES PRESS

Published in the United States by:
Ulysses Press
PO Box 3440
Berkeley, CA 94703
www.ulyssespress.com

First published in 2022 as I AM AUTISTIC in Australia and New Zealand by Allen & Unwin

ISBN: 978-1-64604-418-4
Library of Congress Control Number: 2022936261

Design by Chanelle Moriah and Megan van Staden
Fonts by Chanelle Moriah
Author photo by Judah Plester

Printed in China
2 4 6 8 10 9 7 5 3

This book belongs to

_____

Contents

How to use this book 10

What is autism? 11

Autism traits summarized 12

Stimming 14

Eye contact 15

Imagination 16

Being literal 18

Sarcasm 20

Implying 21

Nonverbal/nonspeaking 22

Echolalia 24

Alexithymia 26

"Zoning out" or dissociating 28

Rigid thinking 29

Making and maintaining relationships 30

Social cues and expectations 31

Being overly sensitive 32

Toys 34

Hiding, climbing, spinning, or being upside down 35

My reflection...36

Forgetting to eat 37

Receiving gifts..38

Expressing emotion..39

Indecisiveness 40

Object permanence 42

Story memory 44

Verbal memory...45

Special interests...46

Info dumping 47

Traveling...48

Fairness..49

Inappropriate humor 50

Need for rules..52

Difficulties summarized 54

Positives...55

Meltdowns...56

Shutdowns 58

Masking and mimicking 60

Unmasking 62

You are not faking..64

Routine...65

Changes and unmet expectations..66

Surprises..68

Vague plans...69

Executive dysfunction...70

Interest-based vs. importance-based nervous system............72

Completing tasks: neurodivergent vs. neurotypical............73

Multiple expectations..74

Multiple options, choices, possibilities..................76

Too many questions...77

Group work..78

Need for precise instructions................................79

Feeling like an outsider or not belonging............80

Sensory processing disorder (SPD) 82

Sensory overload..84

Sensory diet...85

Sensory regulation tools.......................................86

Sensory issues and clothing.................................88

Sensory issues and food......................................89

Proprioception...90

Vestibular input...91

Interoception...92

Cognitive overload..94

Autistic burnout...96

Supporting someone with ASD.............................98

Socializing 100

Listening..102

Processing conversation..104

Not responding...106

Small talk 107

Multiple topics 108

Empathy...110

Understanding relationships...112

Gender...114

Justice...116

Authority and hierarchy 118

Future-predicting questions 120

Abuse..122

The mental-health system 124

Disability...125

Identity-first language (IFL) vs. person-first language (PFL) 126

"Functioning" labels...128

The importance of knowing...130

Thoughts on "curing" autism...132

Acknowledgments...134

About the author 135

Space for your thoughts..136

How to use this book

The first priority is that you use this book in whatever way is the most useful to you.

But if you'd like some structure, here is my intention and a key for different components.

This book is designed to help you learn about yourself, whether you are formally or self-diagnosed, or if you are questioning whether you might be autistic. It is also designed to help others to understand who you are and why you do certain things.

Throughout this book, I will use identity-first language; for example, "autistic person" or "autistics." If you would like to understand why, please see page 126.

☐ —Use these boxes to mark off the things that relate to your experience.

And that's it, really. Super simple! I hope this book helps you to learn more about yourself and becomes a useful tool to share with others.

Use these boxes to write, draw, or scribble your own thoughts, feelings, or experiences.

What is autisM?

Autism is a neurodevelopmental condition.

By definition, "neurodevelopmental" means it relates to, or involves, the development of a person's nervous system.

Essentially, the nervous system is the communicator between our body and our brain. It controls our motor functions (movement), senses, thought processes, and awareness, and plays a part in our learning and memory. It is also responsible for regulating our internal physical state, such as body temperature.

Autism is a condition in which our nervous system has developed differently and functions differently to that of most people. It involves all aspects of how our minds and bodies work.

AUTISM

traits

summarized

Reduced range of emotions or expressions (see page 39)

Poor story memory (see page 44)

Being literal (see page 18)

Stimming/fidgeting (see page 14)

"Black-and-white" or rigid thinking (see page 29)

Poor or excessive use of eye contact (see page 15)

Anxiety around change (see page 66)

Creativity

15:45:39 Needing structure/routine (see page 65)

Sensory issues (see page 82)

Poor imagination (see page 16)

☐ Echolalia (see page 24)

Are you OK?

OK

☐ Hiding or sitting in small or dark places (see page 35)

Difficulty fitting in (see page 80) ☐

☐ Difficulty picking up social cues (see page 31)

☐ Masking/mimicking (see page 60)

Communication differences ☐

☐ Special/obsessive interests (see page 46)

☐ Sensitivity (see page 32)

☐ Executive-functioning issues (see page 70)

☐ Difficulty making and maintaining relationships (see page 30)

Stimming

Stimming is making repetitive movements, actions, or sounds for self-stimulation or self-regulation.

- ☐ Flapping hands
- ☐ Biting nails
- ☐ Twirling hair
- ☐ Cracking knuckles
- ☐ Drumming fingers
- ☐ Tapping pencil
- ☐ Whistling
- ☐ Humming
- ☐ Tongue clicking
- ☐ Blinking repetitively
- ☐ Rocking
- ☐ Jumping or bouncing
- ☐ Snapping fingers
- ☐ Walking on tiptoes
- ☐ Biting or chewing objects
- ☐ Shaking head
- ☐ Repeating words
- ☐ Scratching

Eye contact

Autistics commonly have difficulty using eye contact to initiate, regulate, and terminate social interactions.

This can be a lack of eye contact, or excessive or inconsistent use.

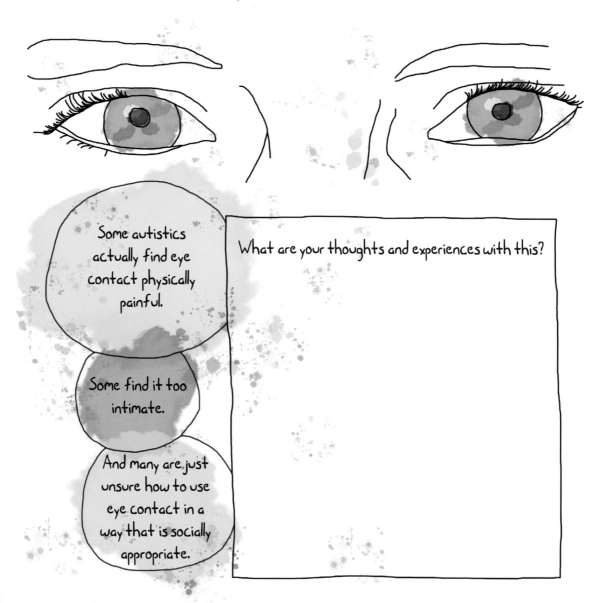

Some autistics actually find eye contact physically painful.

Some find it too intimate.

And many are just unsure how to use eye contact in a way that is socially appropriate.

What are your thoughts and experiences with this?

Imagination

Some autistics have a limited imagination.
Here are some examples of how this might play out:

When handed a set of images or a
picture book, we can find it difficult or
even anxiety provoking to attempt to
create a story based on the images.

When people watching, it can be
impossible to imagine what another
person's life might be like, even if this is
being played as a game.

Pretend play or role-play using toys
can be difficult.

Reading fictional stories may be hard, because
we may not be able to picture the characters or
events as we read about them.

I find using imagination difficult in many situations, because there usually isn't enough context. How can I make an assumption about something when it may not be correct?

Imagination doesn't come with a "correct" answer. It's like taking an exam with minimal information and no time to prepare, then never getting your results back.

Another reason activities requiring imagination might be difficult is that many autistics overanalyze small details. It can take a long time to look at all the details in order to come up with an accurate imaginative idea, and details that don't make sense will slow this process down a lot.

Being literal

Sometimes autistics will take wording in its literal form. This means that metaphors and common sayings may confuse us, and our responses to them may confuse others.

When we interpret things literally, other people can think we are being rude, sarcastic, or sassy, or are talking back. Sometimes we can get into trouble for it and have no idea why.

"What's up?" or "What are you up to?"

What do you mean?

Up is the direction toward a higher place.

Do you mean "What point have I reached?" Because, if so, in what context?

What am I up to in a book I'm reading? I think I should let you know that I'm not reading right now.

"Grab a seat."

Why?

I may be a little odd, but I think you should know that holding a seat makes no sense, unless you want me to take it somewhere. Do you want me to move the seat?

"There's an elephant in the room."

I can almost guarantee that there is not, in fact, an elephant in the room.

Someone once said to me: "Marriage is not a word, it's a sentence." It took me a very long time to realize that it was a joke and not a comment on the English language.

Sarcasm

Many autistics have difficulty picking up on sarcasm.

This can come across as being too serious, but how am I supposed to know what's serious and what's sarcasm in conversation, when they both sound the same to me? I am simply being respectful by taking you seriously.

It's not that we don't find it funny—we may like the joke, but sometimes we need some extra help to recognize that you mean it as a joke.

When sarcasm is directed toward us, it can be very upsetting, because we may not know that what is being said is intended as a joke.

Honestly, though, in many contexts neither party will notice that there was a miscommunication, unless it comes up again later.

Implying

Implying something means to use unspoken language and assume that the listener understands. Many autistics will particularly struggle with implications, because our brains do not function or think in the same way as those of neurotypicals.

Neurotypicals pick up on implications more easily because their brains function similarly to other neurotypicals.

In the same way that autistics might not pick up on implications, we might not use them either.

When I say:

* "Your music is loud."
  I am simply stating a fact. I'm not necessarily complaining or asking you to turn it down. With this particular example, however, it may be that I am trying to communicate that I am overstimulated, but I don't have the words to explain that.
  It's best to ask if I would like something to be done about it.

* "Your house is a mess."
  I am stating a fact, not insulting you.
  I am not meaning to be rude.
  I probably don't care that it's a mess.

When you say:

* "Your room needs to be cleaned."
  I won't automatically know that you are suggesting that I clean it.
  I hear you stating the fact that you think my room could be cleaned.

* "Do you have a spare pen?"
  I might think "Yeah, I have a spare pen."
  I may not realize that you want the pen, because you didn't say that.

Nonverbal/nonspeaking

It is fairly well-known that some autistics are either completely or mostly nonverbal or nonspeaking.

It is less well-known that sometimes even verbal autistics can have times when they are unable to speak out loud.

As someone who is usually verbal and spoken, when I become nonverbal or nonspeaking, it's not the same as choosing not to speak. When I am nonverbal or nonspeaking, I physically cannot get myself to talk. That doesn't necessarily mean that I don't want to communicate or socialize, it just means that I might need to do it differently.

** Note: Different people have different understandings about what the terms "nonverbal" and "nonspeaking" mean.

For some, "nonverbal" refers to those who are unable to communicate using words of any kind, including written words (although they may still communicate using sounds or gestures/movements). Meanwhile, "nonspeaking" refers to those who are unable to communicate using words spoken aloud but who may use words through writing, sign language, digital devices, cards, or other means.

For others, "nonverbal" just means "not expressed orally." In that case, people might use "nonverbal" to refer to times when they do not communicate using their voice but they are able to communicate by other means—similar to the above definition of "nonspeaking." They would consider writing, signing, or using digital devices to be another form of speaking, so they would not use the term "nonspeaking" for people who are able to communicate in that way.

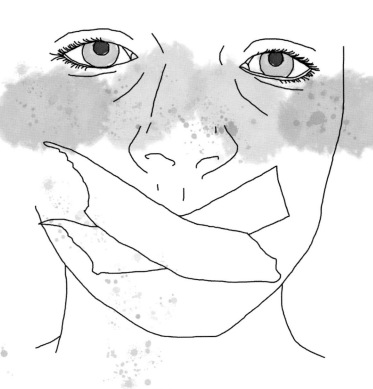

Echolalia

Echolalia is repeating words, sentences, or sounds spoken by another person, and sometimes even copying behaviors. This is common for children who are learning to speak, but often lasts longer in autistics.

Echolalia is usually something that happens in the moment—a repetition that occurs immediately after another person has spoken. But some may also experience delayed echolalia, which is when they repeat words or sentences long after they've heard them. Often, therefore, this is out of context.

For me personally, it is not a conscious decision, and I often can't help doing it.

Situations where I might
engage in echolalia

☐ As another form of stimming (see page 14).

☐ I'm processing a conversation or social situation that I've been in.

☐ I'm trying to communicate something but cannot form the words.

☐ I'm overwhelmed or overstimulated.

☐ I am observing social patterns and learning them, so I can fit in better.

☐ I am trying to engage in conversation.

☐

☐

☐

Alexithymia

Alexithymia is a difficulty with identifying or describing emotions. It may feel as though there simply isn't the vocabulary to describe how you are feeling, or as though you just don't know what you are feeling. It also means that you may have difficulty with expressing emotions that are appropriate to the social setting.

One thing I've noticed for myself is that when I'm asked about how I'm feeling, if I don't know, then I'll make assumptions about my mental state based on different physical factors from my day. So my answer to "Have you been overstimulated today?" might be "I don't know, but I was home all day." My brain draws the conclusion that logically I *shouldn't* be overstimulated because I was home all day, but I don't actually *know* how I've felt, so I can't say yes or no.

Or it could be "I cried, so that must mean I'm sad" or "I was restless, so that means I'm anxious." These assumptions are often inaccurate and don't take into account that actions can have several different meanings or causes.

Sometimes people tell me that I must be happy because I'm laughing, but internally I don't like the way I feel. This can cause me to think that happiness feels bad.

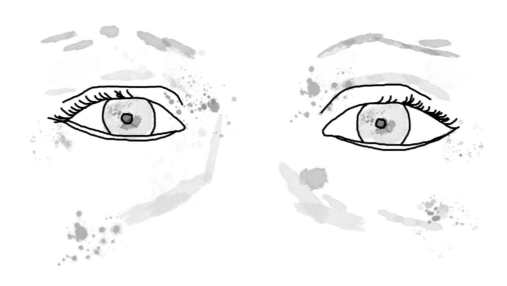

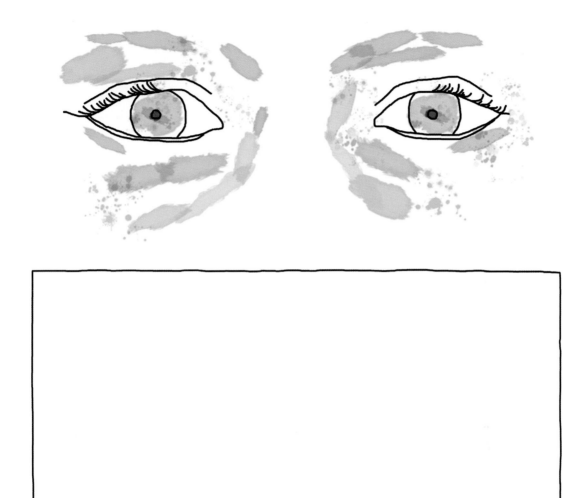

"Zoning out" or dissociating

** Please note that I am not referring here to dissociative disorders. If you experience dissociation, you should seek a professional opinion about what might be causing it.

"Zoning out" is similar to day-dreaming or losing focus. You may not be particularly aware of your surroundings or you may not notice someone trying to get your attention. However, it is usually fairly easy to snap out of.

Dissociating is more severe. It is often described as feeling a disconnection between your body and your mind. It can feel like you have no control over your body—as if you are in the passenger seat. It can also impact your memory and make you feel disorientated.

Both can affect your perception of time. Zoning out and dissociating can also be connected with overstimulation and may then lead to shutting down.

Do you experience this? What happens? What does it feel like? When does it happen?

Rigid thinking

This is also referred to as "black-and-white" thinking.

Rigid thinking is operating under the idea that everything (or most things) has only one correct solution, order, or way of being carried out.

This could be something as small as not being able to wear shoes when you are at home. It could be that the laundry has to be done in a certain way, or at a certain time. But it could also be a belief that if you aren't going to do something to perfection, there is no point in doing it at all.

Individuals who are rigid thinkers are often described as stubborn because they can't easily be convinced to do or think about things in a different way, unless it is something that they have come to on their own. It is also part of the reason that change and unmet expectations can cause anxiety.

Making and Maintaining relationships

Reasons why autistics might have difficulty making and maintaining friendships:

- ☐ Unsure how to interact
- ☐ Unable to pick up on social rules and cues
- ☐ Shy or socially unconfident
- ☐ Difficulty defining "friendship"
- ☐ Lack of similar interests
- ☐ Too many miscommunications or misunderstandings
- ☐ Coming across as intense or obsessive
- ☐ Different communication styles
- ☐ Difficulty dealing with conflict
- ☐ Being unsure if the friendship is reciprocated
- ☐ Inconsistency in interactions

Social cues and expectations

Social cues include body language, tone of voice, facial expression, and eye contact. Social expectations are all of the unspoken rules about what is socially acceptable and what's not. Autistics generally have a hard time picking up on social cues and expectations.

I think one reason for this is that these cues and expectations are inconsistent across different contexts. This can make it really difficult to figure out what different things mean or what we are supposed to do in different situations—especially since we are expected to already or automatically know, and people don't want to explain things to us.

Also, many social cues and rules make no sense. It's difficult to follow a rule that has no logic from our perspective.

Autistics are commonly described as being particularly sensitive in two areas: sensory sensitivity and emotional sensitivity.

Many autistics are particularly sensitive to sensory input. We are often hyperaware of our surroundings. We are not overreacting. Our brains are just taking in more than what others experience.

Imagine it like the volume being turned up on all of your senses—light, sound, touch, taste, and smells all become very intense and there is no escape. Any person would eventually find themselves overwhelmed in a situation like that.

Being overly sensitive

In terms of being considered emotionally sensitive or overreactive, autistics experience a number of additional factors that impact their capacity to handle stress. These include how well they are managing sensory input, how much they are masking (see page 60), and how much they are already struggling with daily tasks or keeping up with their peers, as a result of their autistic traits and difficulties. This means they have less "space" or capacity for stress to be added to their lives before it becomes too much.

Autistics may seem sensitive because they react in a big way to something that you might think is small and insignificant, but it is often just the tipping point. Often the reaction isn't just about what happened in the moment, but more about the fact that there wasn't enough space for them to be able to handle the additional stress.

Toys

Autistics may not interact with toys in the way that is expected. One reason for this is that traditional play with toys requires some level of imagination, which is something that many autistics have difficulty with.

Personally, when given a choice at a toy store, I used to gravitate toward educational toys such as science kits, as opposed to toys that required imaginative play. I used to "play" with my toys by setting them up or putting them in some kind of order or simply placing them in a line for display. I would spend hours doing this and then put them away. Many of my childhood toys are still in near-new condition ten years later.

Most people don't consider this to be playing, but does it matter? I don't think so.

As an adult, playing with toys may still be difficult. Trying to role-play conversations and tell stories through inanimate objects, even when playing with kids, may be quite difficult, or even completely outside of our ability or comfort zone.

At any age, autistics may have a collection of sensory or fidget toys that we "play with" fairly regularly, but this is a different kind of play (see "Stimming" on page 14).

Hiding, climbing, spinning, or being upside down

Sometimes autistics like to hide or sit in small or dark places.

Sometimes they might like to be up high or spin or be upside down.

Sometimes it's a form of regulation or stimming (see page 14).
Sometimes it's for comfort.

Other times it's because they are overwhelmed—
or just because they like it.

My reflection

One commonly relatable experience that I have found in the autistic community is the tendency to stare at your reflection, as well as an occasional lack of recognition of your reflection.

Not recognizing your own reflection could potentially be connected to dissociation (see page 28), but many of the conversations I have had around this suggest that dissociation isn't involved in others' experiences.

I am not a professional—I don't know why I stare at my reflection, or why I might not recognize myself. I just thought it was interesting that a number of people related to this experience.

Forgetting to eat

There are a number of reasons why autistics might forget or even refuse to do things such as eating or going to the toilet regularly. Many of us need to set reminders or make it part of a routine.

It could be because they are hyper-focused on something else. It could be that they simply aren't aware that their body needs something. It could be that they are in the middle of an activity that they feel needs to be completed before they are interrupted by another task. When they are in the middle of one thing or a sequence of things, it can be really difficult to pause and walk away for any period of time.

Suggestions or solutions:

☐ Download a routine app that provides reminders.

☐ Set alarms.

☐ Create associations—for example, after I get dressed, I eat breakfast.

☐ If your child is autistic, allow them to eat "grazing" foods. Healthy snacks that can be eaten without having to step away from what you are doing can be a good option for autistic people of any age.

Receiving gifts

Gifts... they can be really stressful! Not because we don't genuinely appreciate or want the gift, but because of the expectations that can come with it.

It can make us anxious because of the outward reaction that is expected or sought by the giver. When you receive a gift, it often seems like your gratefulness and how much you like it are measured by your outward reaction.

This is problematic, as autistics aren't always good at matching their outward expression to their inward opinion. People's feelings can get hurt, and the more we try to explain how much we like the item, the less they seem to believe us, since our body and face aren't communicating the same message as our words.

It can also be really uncomfortable being watched—for any reason, but especially when you know people are looking for something in your reaction and you aren't entirely sure what that is.

Expressing eMotion

Many autistics don't experience or express emotion in the same ways as neurotypical people. We may feel an emotion without expressing it, or we may express an emotion in the form of another emotion. For example, feeling happy may look like feeling overwhelmed. Or we may also express an entirely different emotion to what we are feeling.

The difference between these two scenarios is that in one the behavior is how we express the emotion that we are feeling, and in the other the behavior is not connected to our inner emotion. It could also be a defense mechanism, if we feel unsafe showing a certain emotion. Alternatively, we may have no idea how we are feeling.

Because this is often our experience with emotion, we also may not read other people's emotions correctly. If someone is crying but tells us that they are okay, we might trust their words more than their actions, and then continue as if that person were okay.

Having said that, some autistics are also hyperaware of how other people are feeling. I guess you could think of it as kind of like how some animals can sense when something is wrong.

Indecisiveness

Autistics may come across as indecisive.
They may respond with "I don't know" frequently and
in many contexts. It doesn't matter how many times
you ask, the answer will be the same.

There are a number of reasons for this. It could be:

☐ There are too many options.

☐ I genuinely don't know.

☐ I have got into trouble for giving
the wrong answer before, and I don't
want to do that again.

☐ I am overthinking all of the factors
and outcomes involved.

☐ I am trying to fit in and I am unsure if
my answer is socially correct.

☐ My mind is genuinely blank.

☐ I need time to figure it out.

☐ I am over all of the questions.

☐ I am having trouble figuring out how
I feel.

I don't know

Object perManence

Some individuals may experience a degree of lack of object permanence. This is your ability to remember things that you cannot see. I am not referring to object permanence in the same way as an infant is not aware that things they cannot see still exist, but it is similar in the sense that if you cannot see something, you might forget about it entirely.

I think this is more common with ADHD, but there is a lot of overlap. Essentially this can be summarized as "out of sight, out of mind." For example, if you cannot see the leftovers in the back of the fridge, you might forget that they exist until it is too late to eat them and they need to be thrown away.

To manage this, a neurodivergent person might keep their belongings in such a way that all or most items are regularly visible. This may seem messy and disorganized to everyone else, but it's best left alone. Unless it is a safety hazard... obviously. If someone else moves or cleans up our items, we can find that really overwhelming, because we may have a hard time remembering what we are even looking for, since we can't see it.

This is also one reason why we may not take the initiative when it comes to tasks that involve other people's belongings. I don't want you to move my things, so I won't move yours—unless you ask me to, and you tell me where everything goes.

This lack of object permanence, unfortunately, sometimes carries over to things like text messages or even people.

Story Memory

Story memory refers to how well an individual can recall a story that they have either read or heard. Individuals with poor story memory may not be able to answer questions in relation to what they have just read or heard. Poor story memory can be misinterpreted as not listening.

This can be a struggle, regardless of age. I am an adult and still have difficulty with this.

I remember a reading test that I had to do regularly between the ages of ten and twelve. I had to read out a paragraph-sized story. The tester would then take the story away and ask me questions about events, characters, motives, etc. This was a test that everyone did, but most other kids did not need to have the story returned to them in order to answer the questions.

I could tell that I consistently wasn't doing as well as I should have been, but I just never improved, because the test required me to be able to recall a story from memory. It wasn't that I was bad at reading comprehension—understanding the story—it was that I lacked the ability to recall what I had read.

Verbal Memory

It is not unusual for autistics to have exceptional memory in some areas and contexts. However, recalling verbal instructions, lists, or lessons may be difficult.

It's not that we aren't listening, it's just that some of our brains struggle to store information that is given in a purely verbal format.

Alternatively, some autistics may be able to recall everything that is said, but not necessarily process all of it. It can be a bit like hearing a foreign language in the sense that the words are just sounds, without meaning being attached to them yet.

In either situation, having information written down or displayed visually can be beneficial.

Special interests

Many autistics have "special" or obsessive interests. These are things that we are particularly passionate about, to a point where it may come across as an obsession. We may gather and store excessive amounts of information on the topic.

There are trends in the things that typically become special interests, but it could be anything. For example, my special interest is autism. I can be absorbed for hours on end, learning things about autism.

I also have a special interest in human biology, in chemistry in relation to medication, and in unusual organisms that I come across.

Info duMping

Info dumping is something that autistics do when they are really interested in a topic. It is usually connected with their special interests.

Info dumping is really just our tendency to talk about our interests, regardless of context or social cues. We may not know when to stop. For some of us, it's kind of like someone has pressed play on an audio file but the pause button is very small and well-hidden, so all of the information comes out whether people are interested in hearing it or not.

Sometimes people just need to be educated, and we are merely doing them the favor of giving them access to correct information. I say this somewhat jokingly but also dead seriously at the same time.

We get really excited when people are genuinely engaged in our interests and want to listen to us spew facts about random things. It's part of how we socialize.

Traveling

Traveling can be a nightmare for some autistics. While (in most contexts) neurotypicals might find traveling to be a nice break, maybe even relaxing, it can be quite the opposite for autistic people.

Traveling often removes routine and familiar environments. It also often comes with unexpected changes. It can be really hard to plan and prepare for everything when traveling. It can be hard to know what to expect, and it often involves some level of spontaneity. All of these things can cause a lot of stress for autistics.

Fairness

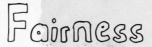

Some autistics have a particularly strong desire for equality and fairness. This may be carried over into seemingly unimportant situations. If that means pulling out a ruler to measure that my brother and I are getting the exact same amount of juice, well into my teens . . . then so be it.

Autistics may be so driven by a desire for equality that it overrides everything else. At times it may seem petty and a waste of time, but in some situations it's quite a positive trait. While some autistics may have a hard time advocating for themselves, they can be really strong advocates for others when they see injustice.

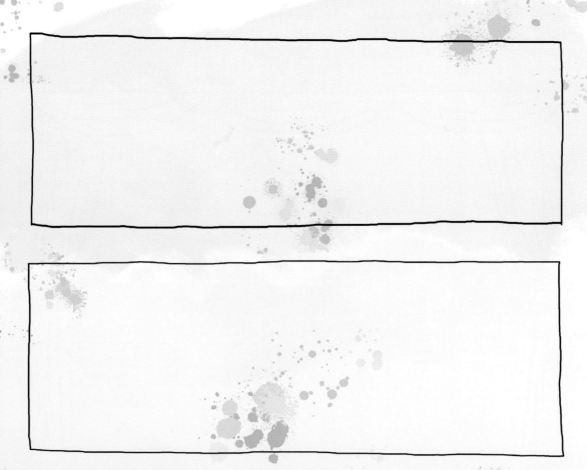

Inappropriate huMor

Quite simply, many autistics are known to laugh at the wrong times. This is partly because we aren't always aware of social expectations, but also partly because our sense of humor is often quite different to most people's.

Picture this: you're at the movies, and everyone is crying actual tears of sadness... except for me. I'm sitting there laughing so loudly that people have turned to look at me. (In my defense, I genuinely thought it was a joke because of how unrealistic it was, and I did not understand why other people were upset.)

Another thing I have noticed is that autistics are less likely to find things funny if they don't make logical sense. They might hear a joke and immediately jump into explaining why something in the joke was incorrect, without realizing that it was a joke.

Need for rules

Many autistics will want and seek out rules in settings that most others don't. It could be because we don't naturally pick up on social cues and expectations, so without rules we can find ourselves in unwanted and confusing situations. Rules are needed to make sense of things, while also keeping us out of trouble.

We might want rules for play, for routine tasks, for different social situations, etc. It's really hard for us to keep up if rules aren't set, because things will keep changing, and somehow everyone else will know what those changes are without discussing them.

At the same time, though, the rules need to be logical. If they don't make sense, they can be really hard to follow.

On this topic, many of us are more than happy to stick to any boundaries you set, but you need to be clear about them. Boundaries help us to know when we are overstepping or being annoying.

If you don't want me to text you on a certain day, tell me that. If you're having an important phone call or meeting and need me to be quiet, instead of saying "I'm on the phone" or "I'm in a meeting," say "I'm on the phone, so I need you to be quiet." I can see that you're on the phone, but I don't necessarily know what that means for me unless you say you need me to be quiet.

Instead of hinting that you need to be somewhere else or that you are having a busy day, just say that you need to leave. In return, please also respect me when I say that I need to leave.

And don't say "It'll only take a minute" or "Just one more second" because, frankly, no one uses those phrases in a literal sense. Just say what you mean.

DIFFICULTIES
suMMarized

Autistic burnout ☐
(see page 96)

☐ Meltdowns and shutdowns
(see pages 56 and 58)

☐ Masking
(see page 60)

☐
Dealing with change
and unmet expectations
(see page 66)

☐ Executive dysfunction
(see page 70)

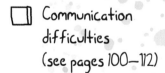
☐ Sensory processing disorder
(SPD—see page 82)

☐ Communication
difficulties
(see pages 100–112)

☐ Poor proprioception
(see page 90)

☐
Poor interoception
(see page 92)

☐ Difficulties with socializing (see page 100)

☐ Trouble processing
conversations
(see page 104)

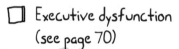

+ Positives +

Here are some positive traits that often come with being autistic, in my experience.

Note that everyone's experiences are different. If you don't relate to these, I encourage you to figure out what autistic traits or experiences you have that are positive. Autism is a large part of a person's identity, and viewing it entirely negatively will hurt you in the long run.

- ☐ Honest
- ☐ Logical/analytical
- ☐ Full of fun facts or information about their special interests
- ☐ Unique (being different is what allows space for new ideas, inventions, solutions, and more)
- ☐ Organized (in their own unique way, perhaps!)
- ☐ Has an equality mindset
- ☐ Accepting
- ☐ Creative
- ☐ Open
- ☐ Says what they mean
- ☐ Loyal

- ☐ Pays attention to detail
- ☐ Punctual
- ☐ Has a strong sense of justice
- ☐ Determined

Meltdowns

A meltdown, in relation to autism, is an uncontrollable outward explosion of emotion as a reaction to built-up stress. It might seem as though it has come out of nowhere, or as though it is an overreaction to one or more present triggers. But the present triggers are often just the tipping point—the thing that causes the bucket to overflow after a buildup of other stressors.

Meltdowns are often mistaken for tantrums and misbehavior. The difference is that a meltdown isn't seeking to gain anything. The autistic person is not doing it in order to get their own way. Meltdowns, in the moment, are the only way to release that built-up stress. They are not a choice.

A meltdown can be very distressing for the individual going through it. The autistic is not trying to make anyone look bad, and the meltdown is not a reflection of bad parenting.

Meltdowns can involve yelling, kicking, screaming, hitting, and other violent behaviors, so it is important to ensure that no one is getting hurt. But otherwise, once a meltdown has started, I personally think it's best if no one tries to force it to stop. Offer the autistic person coping mechanisms and sensory tools. Be empathetic, caring, and provide a safe space, but don't be surprised if the meltdown just needs to run its course.

Shutdowns

Shutdowns are another way that autistics may cope with an overload of stress. Like meltdowns, shutdowns aren't always controllable. They may involve hiding, curling up, or not talking. Some autistic people may simply lie or sit on the floor, regardless of their current surroundings. Often they may not be able to engage in whatever task or activity they were doing until they come out of being in shutdown.

Again, shutdowns are often a reaction to a buildup of stress and may just need to happen. In most cases, being allowed time and space is the best way to recover. Sometimes other people may be able to draw us out by engaging in our interests or offering tools to cope with the situation.

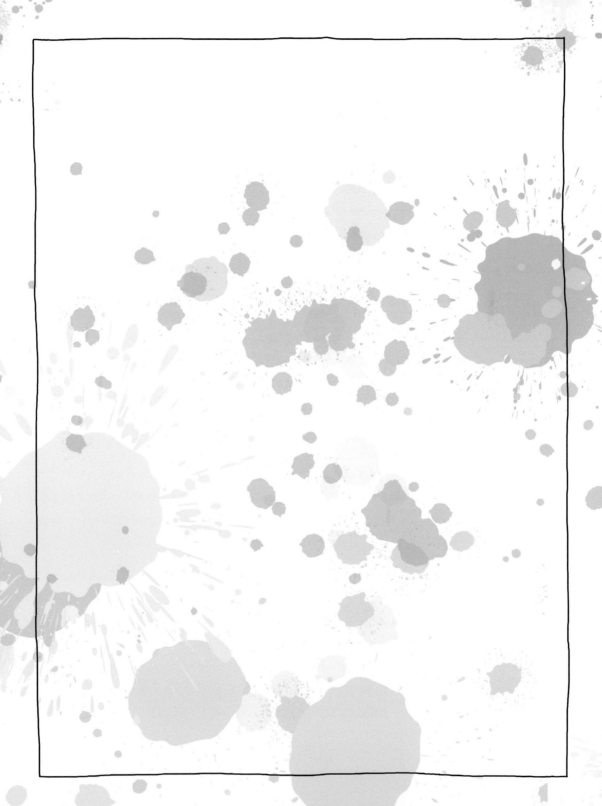

Masking and Mimicking

Masking is the act of hiding your autistic traits in order to live in a world that functions around neurotypicals.

I am constantly aware of every aspect of what my body is doing, how I'm positioned, the tone of voice I'm using, the amount of eye contact I'm making, what gestures I'm using, what emotions I need to show on my body and my face, how much I'm talking, etc.

Sometimes autistics are also trying to figure out what social cues are being put out so we can act accordingly. Sometimes we are so focused on all of these factors and on trying to look like we are engaged and listening that we don't have the headspace to actually listen. Many of us would be more comfortable making no eye contact, using no gestures, and not worrying about our facial expressions or what emotions others think we are expressing.

For me, the easiest form of masking is mimicking. Basically, I'll just copy the person I am with—the way they are talking, sitting, moving, their tone, gestures, etc.

We mask to make others comfortable and to avoid miscommunications that can create some really difficult situations. But masking is exhausting, and it consumes a lot of brain space. It's like being a full-time actor who's been put on the spot, performing live and with no script.

Some autistics will actually create "scripts" for different settings. It is fairly normal for people to think about what they might say in different contexts and to mentally rehearse social scenarios, but the extent to which a neurodivergent person does this can be far more extreme. I know I can spend hours planning, rehearsing, and refining lines and responses for different situations and conversations. I will memorize upward of two thousand words, just to be sure that I get things right, especially if I know I'm going to be in a new situation.

Some autistics even plan entire conversations in their head to prepare for general and specific social situations. This consumes a huge part of our brain space, and it can mean we are thrown off if we find ourselves in a situation that we have not prepared for.

If people were more understanding of how autistics communicate, this would be less of an issue. I want to just be myself—I don't want to have to put on a performance so that others won't misinterpret my body language or words.

Unmasking

Once you realize that you have been masking, you may also realize that you are unsure what it looks like to stop. If you've been doing it for most of your life, it can be hard to figure out what's you and what's masking. It can be difficult to turn off the constant thoughts that you've possibly only just realized aren't a universal experience. Yes, people do socialize without thinking about every detail of what they are doing... somehow!

Navigating how to explain these concepts to different people in your life, and dealing with their reactions, can also be difficult. They may take some time to relearn what different things mean when they are communicating with you. For example, that a lack of eye contact doesn't imply a lack of interest.

Unmasking can take a bit of trial and error, while you figure out what is the most comfortable and least draining way for you. For many autistics, masking is extremely exhausting and it can have a negative impact on overall well-being. So unmasking and being yourself is really important.

You are not faking

This is a common conversation among late-diagnosed autistics. Once they get diagnosed some time in their late teens or early adulthood, they then start feeling as if they are becoming "more autistic," and in turn feel like they are faking it.

If this is you, you aren't faking it.

Most people get to spend those years figuring out who they are, changing from day to day, trying new things, making mistakes, etc. But you didn't get to do that because you didn't know about this huge part of who you are. You probably knew you were different somehow—maybe you felt like you just hadn't found your place yet. Maybe you just needed to work harder to fit in.

You didn't get to spend that time figuring out who you truly are. Now you have the information and you are playing catch-up. You're trying less to be something that you're not, subconsciously or consciously. You are not becoming "more autistic"—you are doing the things that make you who you are, and the things that make life a little more manageable.

Routine

Having a routine or schedule is really important for many autistics. It creates a sense of stability and familiarity. It also helps us to remember to do tasks, including eating or using the toilet. It creates a time and a place for everything, so that we aren't constantly thinking about all the things that need to be done. It also helps us to know when we need to allow time to regulate, or when we will get to do the things we want to do.

A routine is something that is consistent and reliable when the rest of the world is not. Overall, having a routine and a schedule reduces stress and increases our capacity to handle other stressors. There are some really good visual scheduling apps that can be helpful. The one I use is called Tiimo.

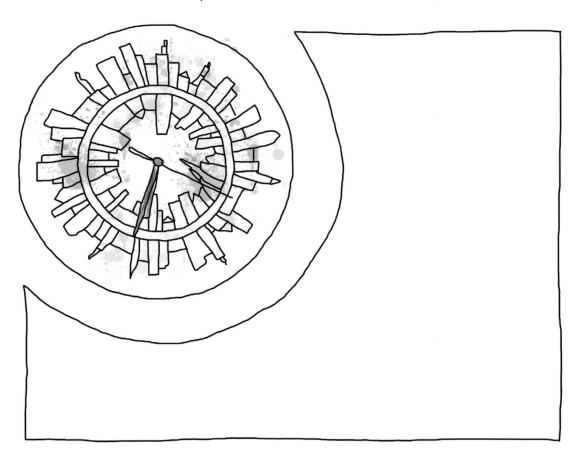

Changes and unMet expectations

For many autistics, just one unexpected change in a day can set off a chain reaction of things that will no longer go according to plan. For many of us, routines and plans are all built on each other. If someone cancels a plan when the day has already started, that throws everything off, and it can be really stressful to deal with.

For some autistics, that window of time is much larger. For me, if I know about a change at least the day before, I can make a new plan—some others can't do that. However, if too many things change in a week, I simply won't cope.

Changes can also be problematic for routines. If one aspect of a routine is changed or can't be completed, an autistic person may have difficulty doing the routine at all. This includes small details like object placement, the food we eat, the people we see, and so on.

I think a large part of why change can cause so much anxiety for autistics is because we have to do more mental preparation than most people. If we aren't given enough time to prepare for something, then, generally speaking, either we won't have the tools or capacity to deal with it or it will result in our needs not being met.

To expand on that, I am an extrovert, so I need a certain amount of time around people. But I'm also autistic, with sensory processing disorder. So if I know I have social time coming up, I will need to take time in my day to be alone, without stimulation. If the person then cancels the social event, I've now spent the day alone, not getting the social time that I need.

It's the same if I am relying on someone to help me with groceries or a chore. If they cancel, I won't have had the time to prepare my brain to do those tasks alone, and then I may not be able to do them at all.

In general, the world is confusing and difficult to navigate, so it's nice if some parts of our lives are predictable and familiar.

Surprises

Simply put, if I am not expecting something, I am not prepared for it. If I am not prepared, I can't be expected to give a reaction that is socially appropriate (from a neurotypical perspective) or an accurate communication of how I feel. There is a decent chance that my unfiltered reaction may offend some people or be taken the wrong way, because I haven't had the chance to translate it into something that you might understand. It may also cause me to become anxious or overwhelmed if I am not mentally prepared or if it changes something that I was relying on.

Vague plans

When I say "vague plans," I am referring to a plan for which a time, place, and other details haven't been decided. Many autistics will find vague plans quite stressful, as they don't allow them to mentally prepare. Also, on the day of the plan, if details haven't been confirmed, autistics can end up in a kind of waiting mode. They may feel unable to do anything else, because they haven't had the chance to make a schedule for it. This can then cause anxiety, because it can mean a lot of wasted time when they might have been able to get more done if the plan had been more firm and clear.

Vague plans are also something neurotypicals tend to use as an easy way to back out of doing things, which, for an autistic, still counts as a change of plan even though the specifics hadn't been set. We may be unable to just go about our usual day and still be ready to go whenever the other person is.

To give you an idea of what a comfortable plan might look like for an autistic, these are the details I usually want: date, time, location, transport, menu (if we are going to eat somewhere new), the expected noise level of the location, and who else will be there.

Please note that spontaneity is different to vague plans. Some autistics may appreciate being invited to spontaneous events, provided no one will be upset if they say no.

Executive dysfunction

Executive dysfunction is wanting to carry out a task but just not being able to. It is common for autistics to struggle with executive functioning, especially if they also have ADHD. It impacts our ability to plan, start and stay on task, as well as stay organized, motivated, regulated, and able to adjust actions according to the situation.

In a sense, what might seem like just one task for one person might become a number of tasks that are difficult to keep in order for someone who struggles with executive functioning. For example, making a cup of coffee (one task) might become: "I want to make coffee. That requires getting a mug out of the cupboard, coffee out of the pantry, milk from the fridge, and a spoon from the drawer. Then I have to boil the kettle. But the kettle is empty, so I need to fill it first. But the sink is full of dirty dishes, so I need to do the dishes. That requires taking the dishes out of the sink to fill it up with water and soap. Are there dishes anywhere else around the house? I need to clean my room" … and so on. By the end of it all, there is so much information and stuff that needs to be done that the original task feels overwhelming and paralyzing.

Even if the autistic person does manage to start the task, information may still be coming through faster than they can deal with it. An individual who struggles with executive dysfunction may start each new task as it comes to mind, while simultaneously forgetting about the original task. This can become dangerous if the initial task was something like cooking or ironing.

Another form of executive dysfunction is when the person is aware of their tasks but unable to prioritize them correctly. All tasks and steps are given an equal priority, which can make it hard to start anything at all. Steps may be approached out of order—for example, going to pour a drink before getting a cup out. Or the person may be unable to switch from the task that they are currently focused on, even if something more urgent comes up.

Some ways to help with this:

* Make a plan for your day or week.

* Make a checklist of things that you need to get done.

* Have step-by-step, visual instructions for tasks that you need to do regularly, and stick to a routine or schedule to complete them.

* Download an app that gives you reminders about tasks.

Interest-based vs. importance-based nervous system

This is a topic that I find really interesting, but I encourage you to do research on this to gain a full understanding of it, because I am not a professional in any way.

Many neurodivergents have an interest-based nervous system, while neurotypicals tend to have an importance-based nervous system. What this means is that for a neurodivergent, motivation to complete a task is triggered by interest. Interest can be created by curiosity, being challenged, a topic they find fascinating, something that falls within their core values, etc. When the interest wears off, so does the motivation. This makes it really difficult for them to do anything that they do not find interesting.

Neurotypicals, however, frequently gain their motivation to complete a task based on its importance: things that are important to them, to their boss, for their goals, for personal gain, or, again, something that falls within their core values. So their way of prioritizing tasks might be determined by what is most important to them at the time.

This can sometimes lead to a lack of understanding between people who are motivated in different ways.

Completing tasks: neurodivergent vs. neurotypical

Here is a concept many autistics might relate to, which is potentially explained by the information on the previous two topics. Often, things that an autistic might be able to do inexplicably quickly, a neurotypical person may take much longer to complete. On the other hand, things that a neurotypical might be able to do quickly and efficiently may take an autistic person a lot longer.

For example, I can finish any assignment to a high standard in a matter of hours, but getting the dishes done can take me up to half a day. This is because I am interested in and challenged by learning and writing. A neurotypical person is more likely to find it much easier to get the dishes done than work on an assignment.

What are some things that you do more efficiently than others?	What are some things that take you a bit longer to finish?

Multiple expectations

Placing expectations on yourself is one thing. But having multiple expectations placed on you by other people can be really overwhelming for any person, autistic or not. For an autistic person, a number of additional factors make this even more stressful.

If these expectations are expressed verbally, we might not be able to remember all of them (see page 45, on verbal memory). If the expectations are unspoken... The stress of this is self-explanatory.

As I have said earlier, we may misinterpret what is expected of us if it is not expressed explicitly. Also, an autistic person may not know how to prioritize these expectations, as our idea of what comes first doesn't always line up with the priorities of our neurotypical acquaintances (see page 72).

Depending on the nature of the expectations, it can be really helpful if they are written out, in order of importance to the people who have the expectations. This makes them clearer and can draw more attention to whether or not they can realistically be fulfilled.

It also means that the person with the expectations can't come back later and say that the expectations never existed. This is called gaslighting, and it happens to autistics way too often. Most of the time they will believe that they must have made things up, which puts them in a position of high stress. They think it's their fault for being unable to somehow automatically know the real expectations, like everyone else— when actually other people just need to communicate better and be aware that their words may be taken seriously and literally by some people.

Multiple options, choices, possibilities

While a neurotypical person may like the idea of having a range of things to choose from, all of their options listed, or the freedom to come up with their own possibilities, an autistic person may just become overwhelmed by multiple choices. For some autistics, having too many options or being asked broad questions can leave us feeling panicked, stressed, and frozen.

For example, something like "What do you want to eat today?" can be too big a question. What are my options? When? What time? At home, or out and about? It ends up being a lot to think about, and as a result we may find that we can't even direct our brains to think about what we are choosing from.

On the other hand, if too many options are listed, especially verbally, it can be too much information. Think of it like this: every option listed is like another internet tab being opened. Tabs are being opened faster than they can load, and the more that get opened, the less the system can manage. Eventually the system may simply shut down.

So, in short, many autistics need to know their options, but not too many at once. Having them written down can be helpful, or having someone help to narrow the list down can make it easier to deal with.

Too Many questions

Being asked too many questions is similar to being given too many options. Sometimes we aren't given enough time to process each question before another one is asked. Sometimes this happens because the person asks several questions in a row before allowing space for an answer. Sometimes it happens because the autistic person needs more time to process what's been said, and their silence is misinterpreted as a lack of understanding or as an indicator that they don't have an answer.

In either situation, the questions are still slowly being processed in the background, and adding more can put the autistic person into a state of overload. This can cause them to shut down completely.

It can sometimes be helpful to check if the person needs more time, or if they are ready to move on. Yes, this is an additional question, so keep it as a yes or no question. If the person isn't ready to move on or they need more time to think, then be quiet. The more you talk, the more there is to process.

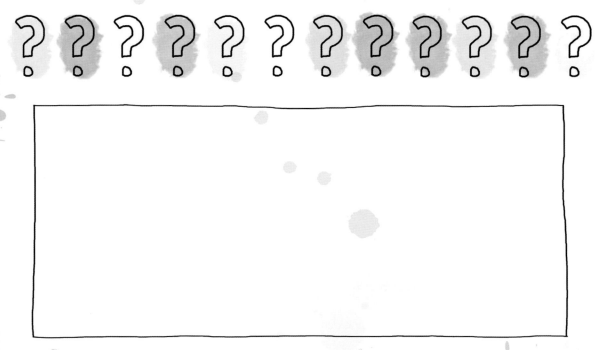

Group work

I'd like to preface this by saying that a lot of autistics can work in a group, but in many situations it can be stressful, frustrating, and far from ideal. Here are some things that can make group work difficult for an autistic:

☐ Having to rely on someone else's timetable

☐ Taking the work a lot more seriously than others

☐ Difficulty with socializing and/or communicating

☐ Other people slowing them down

☐ There is a much higher chance that the end result won't be their desired outcome

☐ Other people not understanding their schedule

☐ Slower conversation-processing speed

☐ Difficulty adapting to changes of plan

☐ Difficulty adapting to another person doing something different than expected

☐ Difficulty with compromise

☐ Others not understanding sensory difficulties

☐ "Why should my grade depend on their work?"

☐ Others don't follow a structure

☐ People going off topic or being distracting

Some autistics may subconsciously try to manage these things by trying to lead or direct the group.

Need for precise instructions

Neurotypicals have a tendency to ask each other for things in as few words as possible, while still somehow understanding what is being asked. It's like collectively they have this silent language that they can all hear, but they seem to forget that it exists—so when they ask an autistic person to do something and the instruction is taken very literally, it sometimes becomes the autistic person's fault for not knowing the underlying expectations and implied specifics.

Autistics often need instructions to be given as literally as possible, without unspoken extras. We are not automatically linked in to the world of things that neurotypicals think are implied or common sense. It might be common sense to a neurotypical, but I'm on a different operating system—it's not common sense to me. Similarly, you might find that what is common knowledge for an autistic may not be so obvious to a neurotypical.

This is relevant to more than just instructions—it applies to explanations, to conflict, to social interactions. In any situation where things may be implied, autistics usually need people to say exactly what they mean. In line with this, most autistics mean what they say in a literal sense. There's not usually any underlying message, unless they are masking and have learned to say things that mean something else.

Feeling like an outsider or not belonging

Most autistics will have a really hard time fitting in anywhere. They may feel like they don't belong anywhere, or like they are on the wrong planet. They may even feel like they don't belong with their family because they are so different to them. This can then mean they don't relate to the feeling of "home" either.

This is one reason why knowing that you're autistic is so important. Belonging plays a large part in a person's sense of well-being. Knowing that you're autistic not only explains a huge number of things, it also makes sense of why you might feel like an outsider and tells you where you might find people who you can relate to.

It also means that statements like "I don't belong here" or "I've never fitted in" can just be our reality. Some autistics genuinely don't experience a sense of fitting in or belonging—ever. It's not just something we've managed to convince ourselves of when we're feeling low. So while these statements can be warning signs of mental distress, they can also simply be an expression of what we go through on a daily basis.

Sensory processing disorder (SPD)

Many autistics will experience sensory difficulties. Some are sensory-seeking and some are sensory-avoidant or hypersensitive. Being hypersensitive means that you experience sensory input more intensely than others do. You might see, hear, smell, or taste things that others don't, and textures can feel more extreme than others seem to experience.

In some cases, the amount of sensory input can be extremely overwhelming (see page 84). Sensory input can even be physically painful. Sensory overload can send an autistic person into meltdown or shutdown.

Being hypersensitive can impact all areas of our lives. Even eating can become an activity that is overwhelming and associated with dread.

Sensory issues can involve more than just sight, sound, smell, taste, and touch. They can also include vestibular input (see page 91) and proprioception (see page 90). I am sensory-avoidant for my five main senses, but I'm sensory-seeking for vestibular and proprioceptive input.

Sensory-seeking is the opposite of being sensory-avoidant. Autistics will seek out sensory input in order to function and regulate.

Both groups can find different sensory tools or input to be soothing. You might be sensory-avoidant and still find weighted blankets, different textures, sounds, smells, and lighting to be soothing. Sensory-seekers will often be looking to engage their senses far more frequently than others, and in more intense ways.

Sensory overload

Sensory overload is a state of feeling overwhelmed as a result of excessive sensory input. A person may not always be aware that the reason they are feeling overwhelmed is because of sensory overload, particularly if it has slowly built up over an extended period of time or if the person doesn't know that they are autistic. The person may be receiving too much information from their senses, noticing things that others do not. This can make everything feel too intense. Lights may be too bright, sounds may become painful, smells can be overpowering.

Hypersensitivity, which leads to overload, is kind of like listening to a piece of music and hearing each instrument and each voice as a separate piece, all at once. Except it's with everything. Every individual sound, flavor, texture, movement, smell, or change is experienced as individual, separate details instead of one combined experience. When this happens too much and there is no escape, it becomes very difficult to function.

Sensory diet

Having a sensory diet basically means using tools to prepare yourself for, and manage or recover from activities that are either over- or understimulating. Sensory tools, stimulation, or lack of stimulation can be used to help you regulate and avoid a state of feeling overwhelmed.

For someone who is hypersensitive, it might mean allowing for time to engage in something soothing before or after an overstimulating activity. Another example is using headphones or noise-canceling earplugs to manage excessive sound. It can involve things like music, quiet, foods, smells, small spaces, being in the dark, climbing, stimming, proprioceptive input (see page 90), vestibular input (see page 91), and anything else that is helpful to that person.

On the following page is a list of different sensory regulation tools. These can all be options for a sensory diet, depending on what works for you.

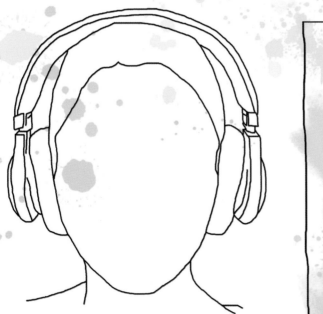

Sensory regulation tools

These are just some ideas—there are so many options. I've made this a checklist in case you're like me and are always looking to grow your sensory collection.

Pressure-related:
- ☐ Weighted blanket
- ☐ Body sock
- ☐ Massage ball
- ☐ Weighted stuffed animals
- ☐ Weighted lap pad
- ☐ Sensory sheet
- ☐ Sensory swing
- ☐

Movement-related:
- ☐ Scooter board
- ☐ Wobble cushion
- ☐ Wobble stool
- ☐ Spinning chair
- ☐ Climbing frame
- ☐

Other:
- ☐ Bubbles
- ☐ Bubble tube lamp
- ☐ Lava lamp
- ☐ Indoor tent
- ☐ Chewelry (soft, silicone jewellery you can chew discreetly)
- ☐ Scented candles
- ☐ Pets
- ☐
- ☐
- ☐
- ☐
- ☐

Sound-related:
- ☐ Noise-canceling headphones
- ☐ Noise-canceling earplugs
- ☐ Rain or ocean drum
- ☐ Music
- ☐ Instruments
- ☐

Fidget-related:
- ☐ Stress ball
- ☐ Bubble pop fidget
- ☐ Play dough
- ☐ Magnetic fidget rings
- ☐ Fidget cube
- ☐ Infinity cube
- ☐ Building blocks
- ☐

Sensory issues and clothing

Depending on the nature of their sensory issues, clothing can be a huge difficulty that autistics have to deal with every day. Tags, seams, stitching, embroidery, rough textures, a tight fit, a loose fit, etc.—it can all become problematic for an individual who has difficulty with sensory input.

It can vary from day to day. It can come on quite suddenly. Some days there's just nothing that works. You may notice that some autistics wear either exactly or pretty much the same thing every day.

My tip for those who struggle with this: have a variety of types of clothes—long, short, tight, loose, stretchy, firm, etc.—but when you find an item of clothing that works for you, buy more than one. Alternatively, you can opt to buy specific sensory-friendly clothing.

Sensory issues and food

Autistics can be known for being picky eaters, for wanting to eat the same thing over and over again, and for eating very plain foods. Meals can become difficult when there are weird or intense textures or flavors, or too many textures or flavors.

Some autistics can manage by having their food separated rather than mixed, and some manage by eating a very limited range of food. Others may do both.

It is important to remember that this isn't just about having preferences and choosing not to eat certain things. It's also not about purposely being difficult or rude. As we have been discussing, some autistic people are hypersensitive, so what might seem mild and manageable to a neurotypical can be extremely overwhelming and distressing for an autistic person. Forcing a child to eat the food can cause a meltdown, which will often get mistaken for a tantrum, and is usually followed by punishment. It is important to listen to why there is an issue with the food, and if anything can be done to help.

As an adult, I'd really appreciate it if people weren't taught that removing things from a meal, or asking for ingredients to be left off their plate, is rude. We are just trying to survive without putting ourselves in an overwhelming situation three times a day—especially when, most of the time, it can be avoided.

Proprioception

Proprioception is the awareness of our body in relation to space and objects, as well as the awareness of how our body is positioned, and how much force we are using. Issues with proprioception can result in clumsiness, bumping into things, being too rough, using too much force, difficulty with motor skills, etc.

It is common for autistics to have poor proprioception, but it can present itself in many different ways. For me, it means that I cannot feel how my body is positioned unless I am touching a stable surface. I know how to tell my body to move into different positions, but I cannot feel the difference between them. For example, if I am in a handstand, having my legs straight and together feels the same as having them bent and apart. I also struggle to tell how tight my grip is, and I often walk into things.

Proprioceptive input is anything that provides intense sensation or input to the muscles and joints. Behaviors that provide proprioceptive input include using a weighted blanket, having a tight hug, walking on tiptoes, chewing, interacting with things that provide pressure (like squeezing into small spaces), etc. It is very common for autistics to find proprioceptive input calming and comforting.

Vestibular input

The vestibular system uses receptors in the inner ear to send information to the brain about head position, balance, movement in space, and changes to the speed at which we are moving. Issues with the vestibular system can result in an avoidance of intense vestibular activities such as spinning or jumping, or it can result in things like poor balance, seeming to never get dizzy when spinning, constantly moving, seeking out more powerful forms of vestibular input, etc. The way in which this presents itself depends on whether the individual is under-or overprocessing information from the receptors in their inner ear.

Vestibular input is anything that engages those receptors—swinging, spinning, climbing, jumping, being upside down, balancing, etc. It is not uncommon for autistics to engage in spinning or rocking, or for them to be clumsy, but having difficulty with the vestibular system is only one possible explanation for these things. Intense vestibular input can also be used as a form of self-regulation.

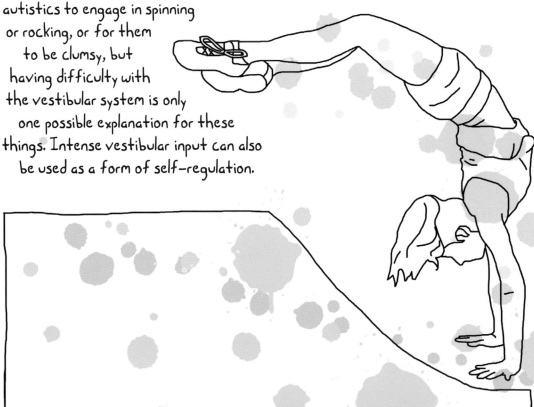

Interoception

Interoception is the awareness of what is going on inside our body. It tells us when we are hungry, full, nauseated, too hot, too cold, need to go to the toilet, need to sleep, etc. Having difficulty with interoception can mean that you don't feel those things, can't identify what different sensations are, or don't interpret them correctly. This can mean that autistics may forget to do certain vital tasks like eating or going to the toilet, or may not be aware of the steps that need to be taken in order to keep their body well.

Some autistics can manage this by having a set routine that includes mealtimes and times to use the toilet or have a drink. Some may need to be taught healthy meal sizes or what clothing is appropriate for different weather conditions.

Difficulties with interoception can also affect our perception of pain, as well as our breathing rate and heart rate.

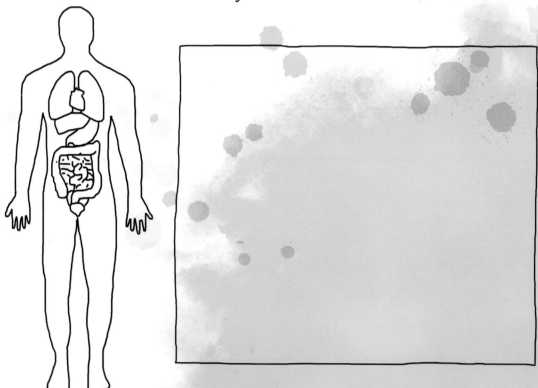

Cognitive overload

Cognitive overload is the term I use to describe the sense of being overwhelmed that builds up as a result of multiple stressors. Cognitive overload can be an underlying cause of a meltdown or shutdown.

Many autistics have a baseline of stress that is higher than that of a neurotypical. This is due to factors such as masking, difficulty with change, difficulty with communication, social differences, and hypersensitivity. The more areas of sensory input there are, the higher that base level of stress can be.

When you add in uncertainty, situations being out of control, multiple expectations, loneliness, executive dysfunction, new things in the routine, vague plans, and anything else that causes stress, it builds up. Autistics don't have as much room for things to be added before they reach a point of overflow. Many autistics can also take longer to process things, so often stressors are coming in faster than they can be dealt with. Most of these stressors are things that autistics can face daily.

One tool that I've found helpful at times is having someone help me make a list of all of the stressors, then going through and making a plan for dealing with as many of them as possible. This can include setting times for sensory regulation; setting a time, place, or action plan for dealing with stressors that can be resolved by an action; or even just receiving an explanation for things that I didn't understand and have been overthinking. But sometimes what is needed is just a break, time alone, or time to recover.

Autistic burnout

Autistic burnout is extreme mental, physical, or emotional exhaustion, accompanied by a reduced capacity for stress of any sort. Given that autistics already have a lower capacity for stress than most people, autistic burnout can make it significantly harder for them to function.

Autistic burnout can be caused by trying to figure out, fit in, and manage the neurotypical structure. Having your needs understood and accommodated, receiving support, and having the freedom to be an authentic version of yourself, without consequences, will reduce the chances of autistic burnout.

Autistic burnout can look like severe mental illness and can include suicidal thoughts and behaviors. If mental-health treatment doesn't take autism into account, it can worsen the state of burnout.

What might be helpful for a neurotypical can be harmful for an autistic person. This is one reason why things like teaching autistics to use eye contact, encouraging masking, forcing verbal communication, punishing them for meltdowns or shutdowns, teaching them to stop stimming, or making them try to keep up with everyone else can be extremely harmful. It's something that neurotypicals seem to celebrate—the autistic person seems more "normal"—but at what cost?

Instead of trying to get autistics to change the outward version of themselves, we should be pushing society to be more understanding and accepting of their differences.

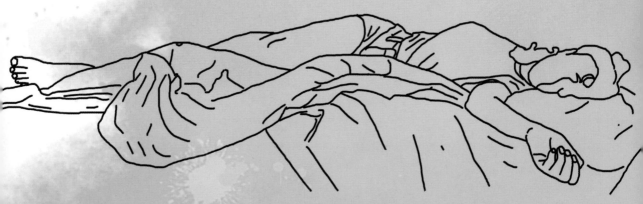

Supporting someone with ASD

Here are some things to be aware of if you are trying to support the mental and emotional health of someone with ASD.

Sensory overload can be a cause of distress. When autistics experience sensory overload, any sensitivities may also be intensified.

"I don't know" can be a true statement. Asking the question again or telling the person that they must know isn't likely to generate a different answer. Telling them that you can't help them if they don't know the answers can also make the situation worse.

Phone calls can be really difficult for autistics. A phone call creates an anxiety-provoking social situation, and it can also be difficult for the autistic person to understand what's being said. Pauses to figure things out and come up with a response are often misinterpreted. If the autistic doesn't answer immediately, the other person can think they're not there anymore or that they're being difficult. It can also result in miscommunication.

Many autistics express different emotions to what they are experiencing internally. It is important to note that outward expression is not always an accurate indicator (see page 39).

Autistics may take longer to respond.

It is important to ask direct and clear questions. When autistics are in distress, there is even less chance that they will be able to interpret and understand questions that aren't to the point.

Withdrawal can be a healthy coping mechanism, as autistics need time to regulate and recover. However, withdrawal can also be a warning sign that something is wrong.

Socializing

This book has already covered a number of aspects that can make socializing difficult—things like avoiding eye contact, being literal, being nonverbal or nonspeaking, not picking up on social cues, having behaviors that are misunderstood, expressing emotion differently, masking, managing change, dealing with vague plans, and more.

However, many of these things aren't issues when autistics are socializing with other autistics. So in some ways these shouldn't be considered difficulties with socialization, but rather differences in how individuals interact.

Understanding, acceptance, and clear communication can go a long way in making social interactions easier for autistic people. Many autistics do need time alone, but that doesn't mean that they don't want friends or social time. Loneliness is a big issue among the autistic community.

The next few pages will discuss more differences in how autistics may interact socially.

Listening

Listening can look very different for autistics. (I find this statement quite funny, because you can't see listening... but you can see some of the behaviors associated with it.) When you say my name, I might not turn my head but I could still be listening. When you're talking to me, I might not make eye contact but I could still be listening. I might be fidgeting, moving, looking around, doing another task, but I could still be listening.

When I respond, my responses might seem unrelated to what has been said, but it doesn't mean that I wasn't listening. It could mean that I made a different connection in my brain and that's where my response came from. It could also be that I heard you, didn't see a need to say anything further, and I've helped to keep the conversation going by starting a new topic.

I could even be wearing headphones or earplugs and still be listening. This just depends on the level of noise-canceling and the reason I am wearing them. A lot of the time, someone wearing headphones and earplugs doesn't want to be spoken to, so it's best to check before starting up a conversation.

Requiring an autistic person to do the things that make you feel like they are listening can mean that they are unable to actually listen. If you are talking to me, you can only expect me to do one of these things at a time:

* Make eye contact OR listen

* Sit still OR listen

* Give acknowledging statements like "yeah," "no," and "mmm" OR listen

If you want me to actually hear and process what you have said, you have to let me do that my way. If you are unsure if an autistic person is listening to what is going on, ask them... nicely. "Hey, just checking that you've heard everything. Would you like me to go back and repeat anything?"

Processing conversation

Some autistics may take longer to process and understand conversation than a neurotypical does. Remember, I am not a professional, but here are some of the reasons that I've heard and experienced for why this happens.

The first is simply that some autistics have a slower processing speed. It's how their brain works. There's probably some scientific explanation.

For some, occasionally, words sound like a foreign language. Literally. You hear the words but they make no sense. This can happen to varying degrees. Sometimes you hear the words but without meanings attached to them. Sometimes the words don't sound like words at all.

For some autistics, it may take longer to process conversation because the autistic person is trying to figure out if they are interpreting it correctly. Sometimes what we hear from an autistic perspective doesn't make sense in the context of the situation, and we can be trying to translate it into what it means from a neurotypical perspective.

Some autistics have reduced thought-space to figure out conversation. For some, there is so much consuming their mental capacity that it just takes a bit longer. This is especially true if the person is hypersensitive and is in a high-sensory environment.

It can be really frustrating in group social settings, because by the time you think of a response or something to add, the conversation has already moved on. People tend to assume that we're shy or have nothing to add, when actually we just need a bit more time to think about it and an opportunity to say what we want to say. Being given an opportunity is important, because many autistics struggle with finding a space to speak without interrupting anyone.

Not responding

Sometimes autistics may take longer to respond or may not respond at all. Here are some possible reasons why:

- ☐ I need more time to process what's been said.
- ☐ I need more time to think about my answer.
- ☐ I don't understand.
- ☐ I've zoned out.
- ☐ I didn't register the fact that you were speaking to me.
- ☐ I don't have a response.
- ☐ I didn't realize that you wanted or expected a response.
- ☐ I've gone into a shutdown or meltdown.
- ☐ I am in sensory overload.
- ☐ I don't want to talk.
- ☐ I've gone nonverbal or nonspeaking.
- ☐ I have had enough of the conversation and no longer wish to participate.
- ☐ I am overwhelmed.
- ☐ I was given too many options or questions at once.
- ☐ I am unsure of how to respond.
- ☐ I've run out of energy or capacity.
- ☐ I have something to say but can't find a space in the conversation to say it.

Small talk

The definition of "small talk" is "polite conversation about unimportant matters." Basically, it is any conversation that doesn't express strong opinions or intense interests. This is supposedly how neurotypicals start to build relationships or trust with other people.

Many autistics do not understand small talk. Frankly, it makes no sense. Why talk about the weather when neither party actually cares about it? It's just talking for the sake of talking. It doesn't bring me closer to knowing who you are, it doesn't tell me your interests or your passions, and, most of the time, the topics are actually boring.

The other thing that doesn't make sense with small talk is that although what is said may be structured as a question, there are usually only a few set responses that are socially expected. Remember that many autistics are not aware of social expectations, so they might answer the questions genuinely and honestly and with actual thought. "How are you?" is the main one. Or something like "Isn't it a nice day today?" The expected answer is always "Yes." Likewise, "Are you looking forward to the weekend?" or "Got any plans for the weekend?" The true answer might not be socially appropriate.

Why ask someone a question when you're already expecting a specific "polite" answer and don't actually care?

Multiple topics

It is not uncommon for neurotypical conversations to have multiple topics and to flow into subject changes. Somehow everyone seems to keep up with what the topic of conversation is and when the changes happen.

For some autistics, this can be really difficult. To us, it's kind of like neurotypicals have multiple chat boxes open. They are able to separate the topics, see when they merge, and know when one's been closed. In contrast, some autistics have only one chat box for the entire conversation. It can then be difficult figuring out how everything that is said fits together—especially because sometimes it doesn't.

Conversation between multiple autistic individuals can look quite different. They may discuss only one topic at a time, moving on only when that subject is finished with. Sometimes that means there's a pause in the conversation, which a lot of us don't mind. Sometimes one person might be reminded of something during a conversation and then proceeds to change the subject, but they don't often carry on discussing the previous topic at the same time.

Please note that not all autistics have this same experience. And obviously, if you have ADHD as well as autism, conversation is likely to be very different again.

Empathy

There is a huge range of experiences with empathy among autistics, and it's not true to say that all autistics lack empathy. There are three things I want to talk about here.

First, let's look at the definition of empathy. Empathy means to understand and share another person's feelings. It means to sit in that space with them and relate to how they are doing. Lacking this doesn't equal a lack of care. Some autistics, like me, have difficulty understanding or relating to emotions or experiences that they have not been through themselves. I cannot pretend to understand, or try to put myself in someone's shoes and feel what they are feeling, because I haven't lived it myself. However, even if I may not be able to "feel" it, if I care very deeply for that person, I'll do my best to do and be what they need at the time.

Hyper-empathy: Some autistics are extremely empathetic. They feel things more deeply than most. However, they may not know how to express that. They may even have a hard time distinguishing between their own feelings and the feelings that they feel on behalf of another person. Sometimes what they feel can be so intense that it causes them to shut down, and this in turn can be seen as a lack of empathy.

Expressing empathy: Many autistics show empathy or understanding by sharing a story of a similar situation that they have experienced. They use their story to provide proof and an explanation of how they understand what the person is feeling. They use it to express the fact that the person isn't alone. Unfortunately, neurotypicals often view this as an attempt to steal the attention, when it's not. It's to say "I know what you're going through and this is how I know. This is why I understand, and I'm here for you."

Understanding relationships

Some autistics may have a hard time understanding or defining relationships or friendships. This is partly because there isn't one set definition for what friendship is, or when you might describe someone as a "friend."

In all honesty, a lot of the time people seem to use "friend" to describe someone they know, rather than to express a relationship. This means that autistics can have relationships where the other person thinks it's a friendship, but it doesn't line up with the autistic person's understanding of that kind of relationship. Alternatively, the autistic person might think they are really good friends with someone, but later find out that's not the case. This can lead to confusion, frustration, and hurt feelings. It can make it hard to trust that any relationship is mutual and result in feelings of loneliness and isolation.

Sometimes when autistics do form a friendship or other relationship, they can be "all in" very quickly. I think the main difficulty with friendships and relationships comes around establishing a mutual connection, a sense of closeness, and an understanding of what that looks like. Clear communication and reassurance can be helpful.

Gender

Research suggests that autistics are more likely than the general population to identify as part of the LGBTQ+ community. But I want to talk specifically about gender, rather than sexuality.

The majority of things that society uses to define and relate to gender are actually just social expectations and are not about biology, practicality, or logic. If we look at the fact that autistics often don't pick up on or follow societal expectations and social rules, it makes sense that autistics would have difficulty fitting into a definition of gender. This isn't necessarily the reason that autistics may identify with a gender that is different to the one "assigned" at birth, but it could be a factor.

Gender is a social construct. It doesn't make sense that one's genitalia should determine what you wear, what you're interested in, how you appear, the colors you like, your hairstyle, what job you're supposed to have, etc. If a person isn't aware of social rules and expectations to begin with, they are more likely to spill out of the mold and be who they want to be, without regard for what others think.
It makes sense that this could then lead to them realizing that they don't fit into what society expects of them as their assigned gender, and coming out as the identity that fits who they are. Changing the label changes the expectations, while also expressing who they are as a person.

Justice

Many autistics have a very strong sense of justice. This was briefly covered on the page about fairness (see page 49). Autistics can have an extremely strong desire for action to take place to fix any injustice that they see. This need can be so intense that it overrides any consequences that may result from stepping in, speaking up, or doing whatever is needed to make things right.

They may have these feelings regardless of whether or not the situation directly impacts or involves them. In many situations, no one is exempt from the autistic person's need to see things be right and just.

This brings us to the topic of authority and hierarchy (see page 118), because often people who feel that they should be more important or more respected can interpret an autistic's sense of justice as disrespect or an attempt to put them below other people. They may then punish the autistic person for trying to make things right where they saw wrong. I think it is particularly common for family members to feel that they shouldn't be "called out," and if they are, then they may feel that the autistic person values them less than whatever is being defended.

In these situations, it is important to remember that it's probably not about you, or a personal attack. It's about the injustice. It's about making things right, and your involvement in the situation is a consequence that's been overridden by one of the autistic's core values.

It is also important to remember that many autistics view all people equally. No one is of lesser or greater value, and that view may extend to family or blood relations. This is less accepted and understood in wider society, where family is often considered more important than other people, and different social rules apply to them.

Authority and hierarchy

Some autistics may have a really hard time dealing with the concepts of authority or hierarchy. Here are some of my experiences with why this is. I'd like to add that while this tendency can cause trouble and be really inconvenient for some people, it can also be really awesome.

From my experience, my brain views every person as equal, regardless of status, age, authority level, race, culture, position, etc. My brain is incapable of viewing any person more highly or more deserving of respect than any other person. There is probably only one exception to this, and that is their level of education. If a person is obviously more educated on a topic, I am likely to place more value on their opinion. However, qualification does not equal education in my brain. People can have qualifications and still seem clueless. Similarly, people can be without a qualification but still be very well-educated on a topic.

Hierarchy doesn't make sense in my brain, and this has got me into trouble at times. Parents, teachers, elders, bosses, managers—they expect a greater value to be given to their words. They often expect not to be challenged, called out, or put on the same level as those whom they view as "below them."

Because I see everyone equally, I don't care what position you are in—I will treat you as an equal. I will love, challenge, and value your voice just as much as I would any other person. Why? Because we are all human, we are all equal.

Future-predicting questions

Some autistics might have a hard time with questions about things that haven't yet occurred, like, "Will you call me if something happens?" "Will you be okay doing this task today?" "What will you do if something happens?" etc. It depends. What's going to happen? Why did it happen? What are my options in the moment? What is going to be the most helpful and effective solution at the time? These are things I cannot answer, because it hasn't happened yet. Another example is "Are you going to be safe?" I don't know. I cannot guarantee anything. I cannot predict freak accidents.

Having to give an answer to a future-predicting question can be really stressful, because things might be different when the situation actually happens. Then it feels like I lied because I didn't do the thing that I said I would do.

It can be really helpful for autistics if questions are worded in a way that is specific and more about the present moment. To give some examples:

* "Here are some things you could do if things go badly. Do you feel comfortable with these options? Do we need to come up with some more?"

* "Do you need any help with this task today? You can let me know if things change."

* "Do you intend to try to stay safe?"

* "Do you feel able to look after yourself today?"

* "Do you know what you can do or who you can contact if you need help? Do you intend on trying to use those options if you need them?"

The main difference in the way these questions are worded is that they're about how the autistic person feels in the moment and about trying rather than guaranteeing. Also, intent isn't definite. Intent is, in that moment, what one is aiming for or wants to do, but it doesn't promise that it will happen that way.

This way of wording may not be helpful for everyone. It's just what worked for me. Some autistics may still find that they are unable to give answers about their intentions because they won't know until the future becomes the present.

Abuse

Many autistics are vulnerable to abuse, particularly of a mental or emotional nature. Bullying is a fairly common experience, for starters. They don't fit in with their peers and often aren't aware of social rules or expectations. They likely have different communication styles or ways of moving. This can mean that they are misunderstood and perceived as "weird," gullible, and easy targets for bullying. By the way, it's not really being gullible—it's more that we take things literally or seriously, and because many of us are very honest, we may trust that others aren't lying to us either.

Beyond bullying, many autistics also have to deal with the world trying to force us to be or act like everyone else, and the ways in which this happens can be unintentionally abusive. It might be over foods or other sensory input and being forced to tolerate something that is extremely distressing.

Abuse includes being punished for a meltdown or a shutdown.

It's being punished for disrespect, when actually we just don't understand hierarchy and are treating people as equals.

It's being punished for misunderstandings or miscommunications, without an explanation of what we did wrong.

It's not being allowed to be ourselves.

It's being gaslit and manipulated by people who take advantage of the fact that we are trusting and are used to being told that we are at fault for misreading a situation.

It's using our autism as an excuse for any hurt feelings, and blaming us when things go wrong.

It's people excluding us because of our differences.

It's making jokes or using sarcasm at our expense when we take things literally and seriously—then telling us that it's our fault that we got upset about it.

It's not being allowed time, space, and the accommodations that we need in order to thrive.

It's expecting us to mask to make you more comfortable.

It's denying emotional support because you've decided that we are too sensitive and therefore we are misbehaving when we express our emotions "too often" or in big ways.

It's causing us to believe that everything is our fault.

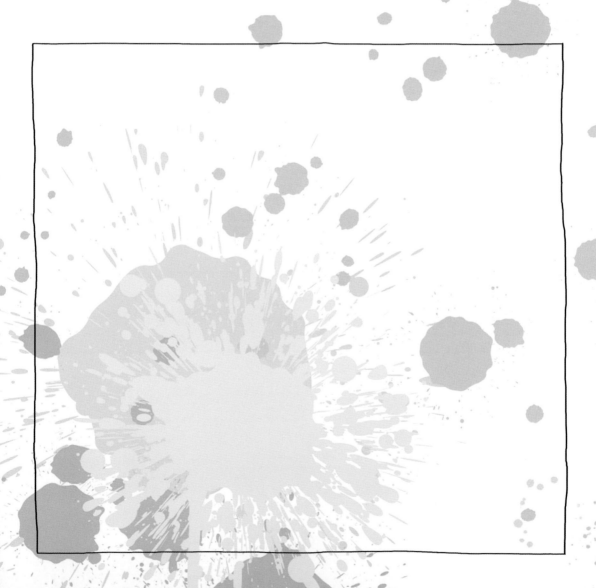

The mental-health system

Engaging with the mental-health system as an autistic individual can be really difficult. For starters, a lot of the time professionals in the mental-health system don't have much of an understanding of (or education around) autism. This is problematic, because helpful treatment for an autistic person is going to look very different to what might be helpful for a neurotypical. On top of all of this, some autistic traits can be mistaken for mental distress by people who aren't educated or aware—things like hiding, not speaking, avoiding eye contact, stimming, having meltdowns or shutdowns, executive dysfunction, and poor interoception, which can look like poor appetite.

The second big issue is that, generally speaking, mental-health professionals are used to treating an illness or disorder to reduce the symptoms. Autism and the struggles that come with it can sometimes be the underlying cause of symptoms of mental distress, because autism affects our thought patterns and ability to manage stress. However, you cannot change autism, get rid of it, or reduce the impact it has on us. Instead, we have to figure out what exactly is causing the distress, learn different coping mechanisms, and adjust our environment to be more suitable.

We may still need support in dealing with distress in the moment and to improve and manage our mental health. But there has to be a different approach, because the mental-health system cannot treat or "fix" autism.

Disability

Let's talk about "disabled" as a label. "Disabled" and "disability" are not negative or shameful terms. They express a disadvantage and a need for changes to be made to accommodate that person. It is okay to allow a person to refer to their autism as a disability, because it is a disadvantage. The world isn't structured in a way that allows us to live a life suited to the autistic brain without some accommodations.

Think about it like this: Let's say one day 99 percent of the population suddenly developed the ability to fly. Then, because most people can fly, a large portion of society's structures and daily tasks start requiring the ability to fly. Those who never developed that ability are now at a disadvantage. They are now disabled. That doesn't make them any less valuable or able than they were before things changed, and saying they are disabled isn't an insult. It just means that they now require certain accommodations in order to do the things that everyone else is doing. In a lot of cases, making accommodations for those who are disabled actually makes life easier for everyone.

Disability just means that you aren't able to do things the same way as most people, and as a result, the structure of society isn't entirely suited to your level of ability. I have a disability not because I'm different, but because of the structure of the society that I live in.

Identity-first language (IFL) vs. person-first language (PFL)

* Identity-first language is saying "autistic person" or "I am autistic."

* Person-first language is saying "person with autism."

Among the autistic community, most autistic individuals prefer identity-first language. On the other hand, parents, professionals, and other neurotypicals prefer, and are taught to use, person-first language—even though it's not about them.

Many autistics view person-first language as harmful or ableist. PFL implies that the person's autism is something that is viewed extremely negatively. It almost tries to separate the person from their autism, from identifying with it. Think about it: you wouldn't say "person with extroversion," "person with competitiveness," "person with selfishness," or "person with laziness."

We allow both positive and negative labels about people's personalities and identities. Autism is a much larger part of who we are: it affects not only our personality but also our movements, our thought patterns, our way of being. Autism is the way in which my brain is wired; it is who I am. I don't just carry it with me, and I am not separate from it.

We use PFL for illnesses, things that are wrong with a person's well-being. "Person with cancer," "person with dementia," "person with the flu." Autism is not an illness. It's not something that's wrong with me. It's a different neurotype.

By saying that a person should use only PFL, you're also saying that if you can't identify with the neurotypical neurotype then you shouldn't identify with a neurotype at all. Now, I know most people don't say that they are neurotypical—heck, most of them don't even know the word. But I can guarantee that if they did, they wouldn't be told to say "person with a neurotypical neurotype."

I am autistic, and I love that about me.

"Functioning" labels

When I say "functioning" labels, I am referring to the terms "high-functioning" and "low-functioning." Many people in the autistic community view these terms as ableist, invalidating, and not an accurate reflection of anything other than how well we "pass" in the neurotypical structure.

When someone says that an autistic person is "high-functioning," most of the time it's trying to express how "normal" an autistic person appears to be. It's not representative of their needs, support requirements, or differences. It's often phrased as "Oh, you're autistic? But you're high-functioning." Saying that someone is high-functioning is used as a quick pass to disregard all of their experiences and differences as an autistic individual.

Autistics can get labeled as high-functioning regardless of whether or not they need support in certain areas. This label can then prevent them from getting the support that they need. Calling someone "high-functioning" is simply saying "You can, at the very least, look like you are functioning in a neurotypical world. That makes others more comfortable, and you are expected to keep doing that even if it is forcing you into burnout. We are not likely to provide as much support or accommodation because you are able to mask to fit into our world."

On the other hand, "low-functioning" is used very negatively. I've mostly seen it used to express how difficult it makes life for those who support the individual. It isn't reflective of the person's strengths or what their support needs actually are. It refers to those who are unable to pass or function in a neurotypical structure.

Autism and the needs associated with it can vary significantly from one person to another. It doesn't make sense to have only two labels that express how autism affects people, and the labels shouldn't be about how well they can hide their autism.

Fortunately, functioning labels are being done away with. Instead, we should be talking about what support needs the person has, the accommodations they require, and their strengths and differences associated with being autistic.

The importance of knowing

This topic is about the importance of getting a diagnosis as early as possible, as well as the importance of someone being aware of their autism from early on.

For the well-being of an autistic individual, it is essential that they know about their autism from a young age. No one is being protected by avoiding this awareness. Imagine it like this: Let's say you're blind. Except you don't know that you're blind, and neither do most people. You know that you're different, but you don't know why. You have a hard time doing things that others find easy, and no one understands why you can't just get it together, figure things out, and keep up. You feel like a failure because you don't know that everyone else has an advantage that you don't have.

On top of that, since people don't know that you're blind, you also don't get access to tools to make things more manageable and fair. So you spend excessive amounts of energy trying to look like you're not struggling, like you're not different from others. You don't learn how to do life in a way that works for you, because you are trying to do it like everyone else. In the process, you're draining yourself and constantly feeling inadequate. If you had known you were blind, you could have had the right tools, support, and information. You could have found others who understood your experience, who didn't look down on you for it, and who weren't trying to "fix" you.

Now imagine this: instead of blindness, it's something that affects your thought patterns, your movements, your ability to manage stress, your social skills, the entire way your brain works. Autistics know that they are different, regardless of whether they know about their autism or not. They know that they are struggling and becoming increasingly tired every day, but unless they know that they are autistic and what that means, they don't know that their peers aren't having the same experience. Eventually they will burn out because they don't have the capacity to keep trying to keep up with everyone else when they don't have the same advantages.

As someone who was diagnosed at the age of twenty-one, I feel that knowing sooner could have prevented or reduced the seven years of severe mental illness and safety concerns that I went through. I felt alone and completely out of place. It was only after my diagnosis that I started finding places where I felt a sense of belonging and people understood me. I was also given access to supports and information that could help me to actually manage life.

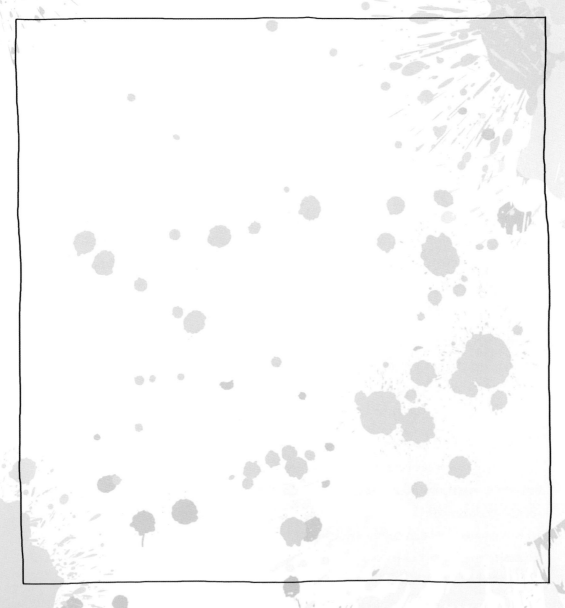

Thoughts on "curing" autism

I'm going to preface this with a reminder that you can't cure autism. And here are my thoughts on the idea of working toward a "cure."

If we look at the fact that autism is a neurodevelopmental condition, the fact that it impacts the way our body and brain develop and the way we perceive and understand the world, we should realize that autism changes and forms who we are as a person. To cure a person's autism would be to completely change who that person is.

On top of that, the autistic person has spent their life developing and perceiving and understanding life in one way. If that suddenly changed, it would be extremely confusing and traumatic. It would affect all of the person's memories up until that point, and they would have to relearn their entire understanding of life.

So let's say that instead we look at curing specific autistic traits. Currently, with many autistic traits, a person might look as though they've been cured, but they have probably just learned how to mask, which can be detrimental to their well-being in the long run. Some autistic traits actually help the individual to regulate. Taking those tools away puts them in a position where they are trapped, with a growing sense of being overwhelmed that can lead to burnout.

With many autistic traits, there is no *need* to try to fix them. They aren't harming anyone, and all that's really needed is understanding and acceptance. Opting for curing over understanding is ableist. A number of traits that might cause a person problems can also be helped with some accommodations.

Moving on, if we look to cure autism by preventing the birth of autistic individuals, then we start getting into eugenics and discrimination. Life has difficulties for autistics, mostly because the world isn't educated about autism, or understanding and accommodating of it. Raising a child with a different neurotype brings its challenges, but raising any child can come with unexpected struggles. As an autistic individual, I find it easier to connect with and look after autistic children, but that doesn't mean I'd want to avoid having a neurotypical child.

Looking at all these points, I can't think of any good reason to try to rid the world of autism. As someone who was diagnosed late and spent twenty-one years suppressing my autistic traits to fit in—resulting in several years of burnout and suicidality—I much prefer my life now, where I am free to be the authentic, autistic version of myself. There is nothing that would make me want to cure my traits, because in a way I've already been there (or as close as one can get to it) and it put my life at risk.

Just let us be.

Acknowledgments

I would like to acknowledge the staff at Autism NZ, who have been really supportive of me in my own personal autism journey, as well as instrumental in my book making it this far. I specifically want to acknowledge Megan McNeice, who pushed me to submit the book to be considered for publication. Megan shared my work with Claire Mabey and Andrew Laking from Verb Wellington, and from there it was sent on to Allen & Unwin. I want to acknowledge Ben Martell for taking the time to go through and correct many errors in the manuscript before I signed with the publisher. Thank you to these people, who saw the value in my work before I did.

When I was first diagnosed, I was given a resource called "Crisis Supports for the Autism Community," published by the American Association of Suicidology, which was useful to me when I was researching autism and making notes for this book (in particular the material on feeling like you don't belong and on supporting someone with ASD). I also found the UK website Autism Together (autismtogether.co.uk) helpful in understanding proprioception and vestibular input. I am thankful, too, for the hundreds of autistics who answered numerous questions I had along the way as I aimed to make this book as inclusive as possible.

I also want to thank my publishing team at Allen & Unwin. They have all done an amazing job of adapting to working with me as an autistic person. My publisher, Michelle, has been encouraging right from the start, and extremely helpful in explaining all of the processes along the way. Megan has done a lovely job of editing the design and layout, especially given my aversion to change. And Leanne has been very thorough and has made the whole process a lot easier for me. She has tied everything together really well, and I have enjoyed working with her.

About the author

Chanelle Moriah is an autistic author and illustrator who is passionate about creating spaces of understanding to allow the freedom of individual expression. As a late-diagnosed autistic, they are particularly passionate about bringing awareness to the different ways in which autism can present itself and the importance of being able to live your life accordingly. They enjoy creating art in a variety of forms, and hope that if there is one thing they can achieve in life, it's to help other people.

This is Chanelle's first book.

Space for your thoughts